A Volcano Wakes Up

Written by Julie Mitchell

T0352592

Contents

Warning signs

"Mount St Helens is showing signs of **erupting**," my producer at the television station said. "I want you to go there and cover the story."

It was 20 March 1980. Mount St Helens is a volcano in the Cascade Range of mountains in the north-west of the United States of America (USA). I knew it had been **dormant** since 1857 – that was 123 years ago!

"That mountain is a huge tourist attraction," I said. "An eruption would put a lot of lives at risk."

"It's unlikely to happen," my producer said. "But it's worth checking out, just the same."

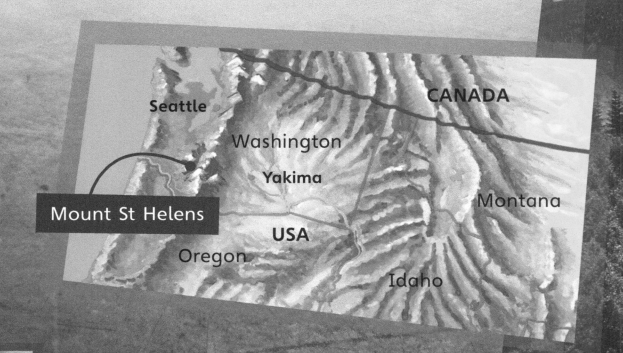

Seattle

Washington

Yakima

Mount St Helens

USA

Oregon

CANADA

Montana

Idaho

Mount St Helens today

Steam coming out of the volcano's crater

No worries yet

I flew to Mount St Helens with my cameraman, Johnny, and started interviewing some local people. Most said they had noticed some small earth **tremors**, but they claimed they weren't worried. I wasn't worried either, until Johnny began filming from the helicopter.

"Look!" he shouted suddenly. "The mountain top's starting to bulge!"

A week later, we flew over Mount St Helens again. Now, long **fissures** were showing in its sides, with steam coming from them. A large **crater** had opened up, blasting out more steam. Then a black cloud appeared, dropping **ash** onto the mountainside.

The mountain was awake

Was an eruption about to begin? Some local people thought so, and they were preparing to leave.

On 10 April, a cloud of steam rose from Mount St Helens. "It must be 300 metres high!" Johnny shouted, focusing his camera on it.

We were lucky that we didn't fly any closer! Suddenly, the mountain began spurting streams of black rock into the air. Then it sent up dark clouds, which rained ash onto the volcano's slopes.

"The mountain's awake," Johnny said, his eyes wide with shock.

"Yes," the pilot replied. "Awake and angry."

A cloud of steam 300 metres high rising from Mount St Helens

A serious warning

The cloud of steam was a serious warning of a major eruption. Scientists couldn't say exactly when it would happen, but they said everyone should leave the mountain immediately.

Over the next few days, the tourists and many of the people who lived on Mount St Helens left. But some people ignored the warning and stayed.

Many people left the area and took their pets with them

Volcanologists observed and recorded the eruption

More scientists and **volcanologists** started arriving.
They planned to observe and record the events
of the big eruption. The ground shook continually
beneath their feet. Although the scientists knew
they were putting themselves in danger, they were
prepared to take the risk.

Was the crisis over?

Now I was reporting from the helicopter every day. I kept expecting to be covering a huge volcanic eruption. But it didn't happen.

Instead, the mountain grew quieter; it was producing less steam and there were fewer tremors. The scientists were still advising people to leave, but by the end of April it didn't seem necessary.

I began to think the crisis might be over. Had the mountain released enough pressure to settle down again?

The mountain had grown quieter

crater

vent

Cross-section of a dormant volcano

The mountain was going back to sleep

By May, everything was still quiet. Johnny and I filmed the mountain from a safe distance every morning, but there was very little to report. It seemed that the scientists had been wrong. Mount St Helens was not going to erupt; it was going back to sleep, just as it had been doing for the last 123 years.

At 8.30am on 18 May, I was reporting from the helicopter again. Suddenly, there was a violent explosion. The whole north **face** of Mount St Helens was collapsing in a **landslide**, sending an **avalanche** of rocks and **debris** down the mountainside.

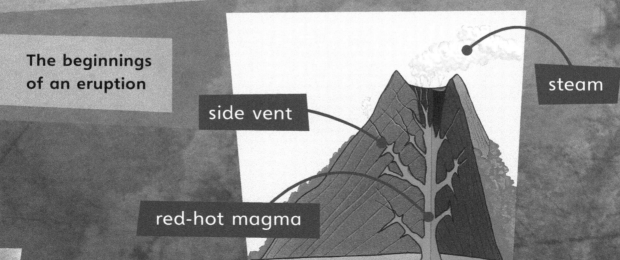

The beginnings of an eruption

steam

side vent

red-hot magma

12

At 8.30am on 18 May there was a violent explosion

Mount St Helens was erupting!

A huge cloud was surging hundreds of metres upwards from the **peak** and another was rising from the landslide. A blast of air flattened some trees near the volcano and knocked down others much further away.

"This is it!" I shouted into the microphone. "Mount St Helens is erupting!" I looked at the mountain top. "About 300 metres of its peak has been blasted away! The clouds of ash and steam are enormous!"

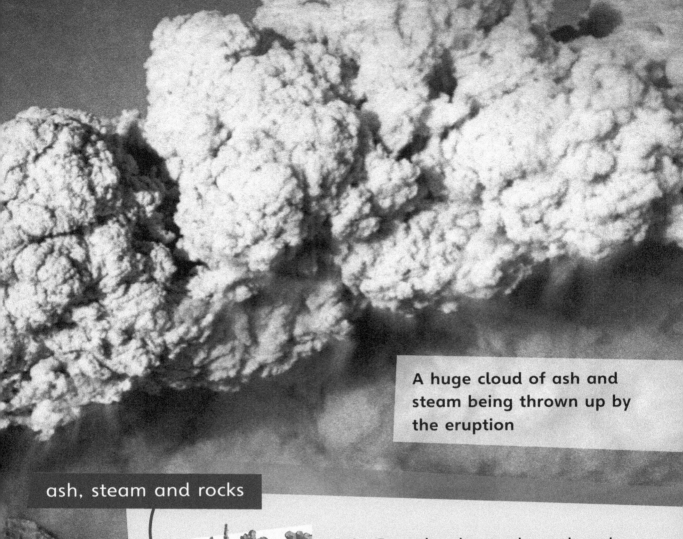

A huge cloud of ash and steam being thrown up by the eruption

ash, steam and rocks

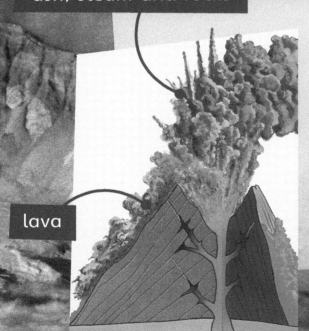

lava

As I spoke, hot ash and rocks fell onto the slopes, starting forest fires. **Lava** swept down the mountainside. It flowed into the rivers and lakes, making them boil and send more steam into the air.

A steaming mudflow

Then I saw that melting snow and ice was pouring down the mountainside from the upper slopes. The water combined with the landslide, making a steaming mudflow that plunged along river valleys.

Trees were flattened in the landslide

I knew this type of mudflow had a special name: lahar.

"It's moving at incredible speed!" I reported. "At least 60 kilometres an hour!"

The lahar grew into a mighty torrent that broke the banks of rivers and carried away boulders and fallen trees. Further downstream, it destroyed roads and swept away houses.

The lahar made a steaming mudflow that plunged along river valleys

The bridge didn't stand a chance

The lahar became thick with **wreckage**. It flowed along the Toutle River and collected logs cut by the forest workers. 50 kilometres below the mountain, it **felled** full-grown trees. By the time it reached the Toutle River bridge, it was a solid moving force. The bridge didn't stand a chance; when the giant lahar hit it, the bridge was simply knocked off its supports and carried away.

The Toutle River bridge was knocked down and buried in mud

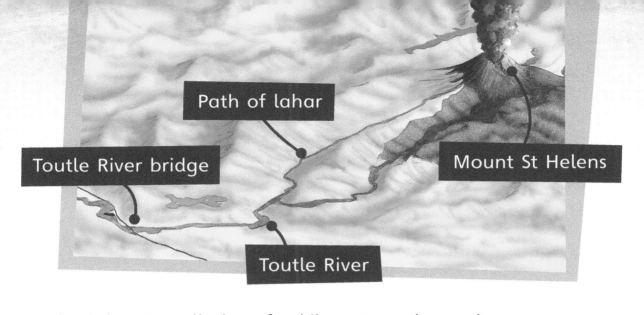

Path of lahar

Toutle River bridge

Mount St Helens

Toutle River

The lahar travelled on for kilometres, destroying more than 200 houses, and sweeping away a huge area of forest. Finally, it spread out over the countryside, burying it in mud more than 100 metres deep.

Ash was falling everywhere

The volcanic cloud hovered over Mount St Helens, dropping ash on everything below it. The cloud grew until it was 33 kilometres high, then it moved off to the east.

That night, we heard that ash was falling in Missoula, Montana, more than 600 kilometres away. Scientists estimate that more than 50,000 tonnes of ash fell from the cloud, some of it landing as far away as Oklahoma.

ash cloud

Mount St Helens

Oklahoma

The ash cloud covered
a huge area

Everyone helped to
clear up the ash

Where were all the animals?

On 20 May, two days after the eruption, Johnny and I filmed the volcano again. "It looks like a **wasteland**," Johnny said as we flew over it.

The top of the mountain was now a huge, jagged crater, and everything within 20 kilometres of it was burned. Trees, stripped of their branches, lay like scattered matchsticks on the slopes. There was no sign of animal life anywhere.

"How terrible!" I said. "I wonder if any of the animals sensed what was coming and got away before it happened?"

"Maybe," Johnny said, "but they're homeless now."

Could any animals have survived after the volcano erupted?

Could the volcano explode again?

As we flew back to the TV station, I thought about the power of the explosion which had sent a huge part of Mount St Helens into the air. The eruption had caused the death of several people and it had destroyed buildings, roads, bridges, crops, forests and wildlife. It had totally reshaped the landscape, too.

Might the volcano explode with such force again?

Only time will tell.

The eruption caused a lot of damage and changed the landscape for ever

Weekend of fiery rioting leaves 19 dead

Oregon Journal
9 die
lost in eruptio
4-page special section

Monday, May 19, 1980   15¢

The Oregonian
Forecast: cloudy; high, 68; low, 50; report on Page C32
22 CENTS
FINAL STOCKS
Dow Jones: up 1.62

98 persons listed as missing

Longview,
Kelso face

Closing Dow Jones: 830.8E, up 4.01; stocks on Page A12

The Oregoni

Mud dams lake, imperils

Mr. X picks
STREET FINAL

Oregon Journal
Thursday, May 22, 1980   15¢

'Worst thing I've ever seen'
Disaster staggers Carter

Volcanic eruptions around the world

Where: Tambora, Indonesia
When: 10 April, 1815

This is the largest volcanic eruption ever recorded, and it killed 92,000 people. 1815 was called 'the year without a summer' because the huge amount of gases and dust made the weather cooler and stopped sunlight coming through.

Where: Krakatau, Indonesia
When: 26 August, 1883
36,000 people died during two days of eruptions. They started after clouds of black ash had been spurting out of the volcano for months. During the final massive eruption, two thirds of the island collapsed into the sea.

Where: Mont Pelée, Martinique
When: 8 May, 1902
A town called St Pierre lay at the foot of the volcano. Although there were signs that an eruption might be coming, important people in the town wanted everyone to stay put so that they could vote in an election three days later. The volcano *did* erupt and 30,000 people died.

Where: Nevado del Ruiz, Colombia

When: 13 November, 1985

This volcano is known as 'the sleeping giant'. After signs of activity, an evacuation was ordered, then cancelled, as the volcano seemed to have grown quiet again. A few hours later, a huge eruption killed 25,000 people.

Where: Unzen, Japan

When: 1792

The eruption itself did not cause severe damage, but a month later landslides swept down the nearby mountain, Mayuyama. They tore through Shimbara City and flowed into the sea. This caused a **tsunami** that killed more than 14,000 people.

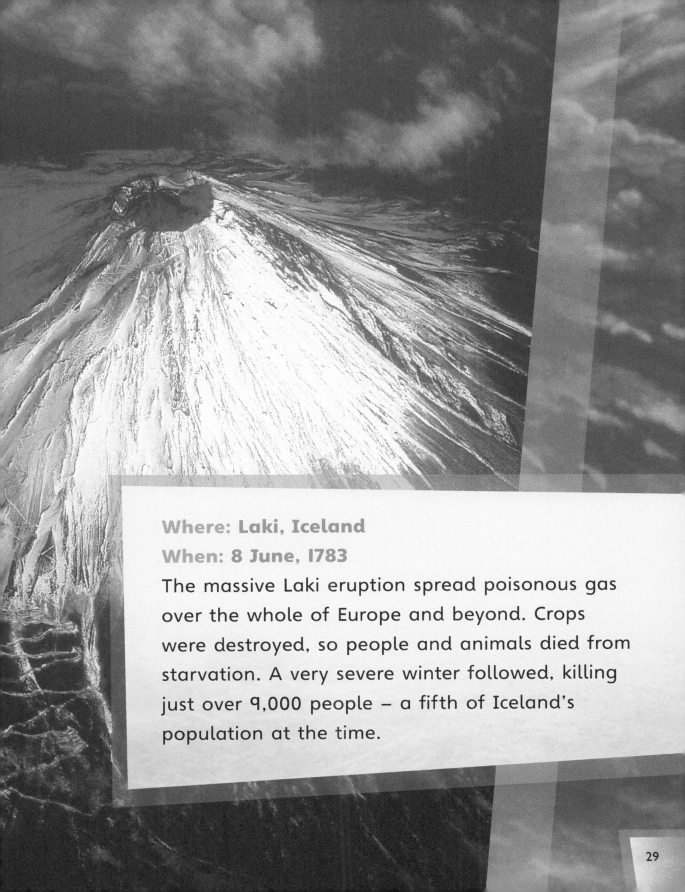

Where: Laki, Iceland

When: 8 June, 1783

The massive Laki eruption spread poisonous gas over the whole of Europe and beyond. Crops were destroyed, so people and animals died from starvation. A very severe winter followed, killing just over 9,000 people – a fifth of Iceland's population at the time.

Quiz

1 Where is Mount St Helens?
   a) India   b) Africa   c) North America

2 When was the last time it erupted?
   a) 1812   b) 1857   c) 1923

3 Who flew to Mount St Helens to cover the story?
   a) a producer and assistant
   b) a reporter and photographer
   c) two scientists

4 Where did the water in the lahar come from at first?
   a) melted snow and ice
   b) rain
   c) a river

5 What happened to the Toutle River bridge?
   a) It stayed upright.
   b) It broke in two.
   c) It was knocked down and carried away.

Answers on page 31

Glossary

ash	tiny pieces of rocks and lava that form part of an eruption
avalanche	sudden fall of rocks, ice or snow
crater	round opening in the top of a volcano
debris	small amounts of broken rocks and other material
dormant	not active
erupting	when a volcano forces out rock, lava and ash
face	steep side of a mountain
felled	cut down
fissures	narrow cracks in surface of rock
landslide	mass of rocks and soil that slides when part of a mountain gives way
lava	magma after it has erupted
magma	liquid rock before it erupts
peak	pointed top of a mountain
tremors	small earthquakes
tsunami	long, high sea waves caused by volcanic eruption or earthquake
volcanologists	scientists who study volcanoes
wasteland	place where nothing grows or lives
wreckage	remains of something that has been destroyed

Quiz answers: 1c; 2b; 3b; 4a; 5c

Index